YOU NEVER APPRECIATE ALL THE THINGS YOUR MOTHER DID FOR YOU UNTIL YOU FIND YOURSELF DOING THE SAME THINGS FOR YOUR KIDS. -LINDA POINDEXTER

Designed by Signature Kisses

my name is

Date of Birth	Place of Birth

MY PARENTS

MOTHER'S FULL NAME

Date of Birth	Place of Birth

FATHER'S FULL NAME

Date of Birth	Place of Birth

MY SIBLINGS

MY PATERNAL GRANDMOTHER

Date of Birth

Place of Birth

MY PATERNAL GRANDFATHER

Date of Birth

Place of Birth

MY MATERNAL GRANDMOTHER

Date of Birth

Place of Birth

MY MATERNAL GRANDFATHER

Date of Birth

Place of Birth

My family tree

My family tree

Photographs

Photographs

WHAT TYPE OF HOUSE DID YOU ·GROW UP IN?·

•WHAT DO YOU REMEMBER ABOUT•
•THE PLACES YOU•
LIVED IN AS
A CHILD?

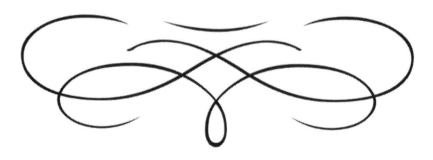

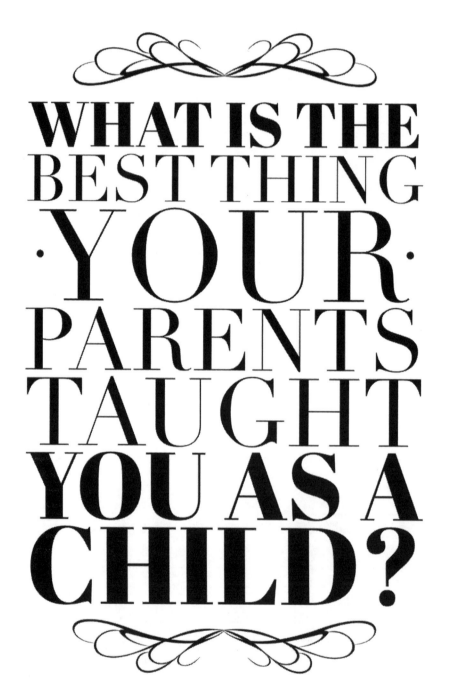

WHAT IS THE BEST THING ·YOUR· PARENTS TAUGHT YOU AS A CHILD?

WHICH ONE OF YOUR ·PARENTS· DO YOU ·MOSTLY· RESEMBLE?

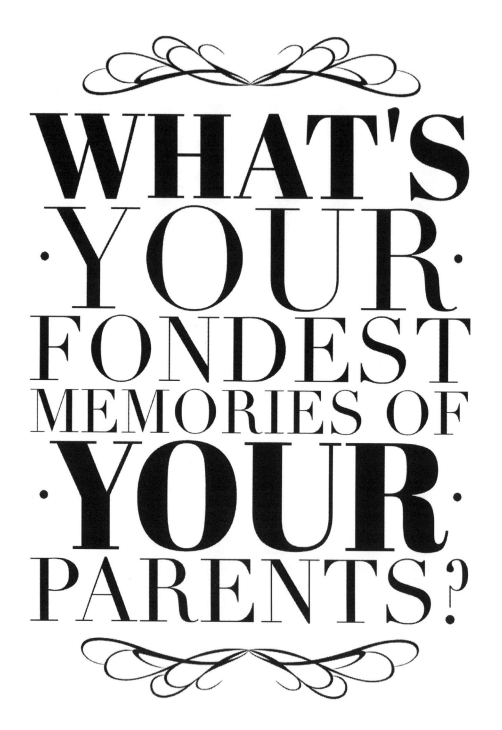

WHAT'S · YOUR · FONDEST MEMORIES OF · YOUR · PARENTS?

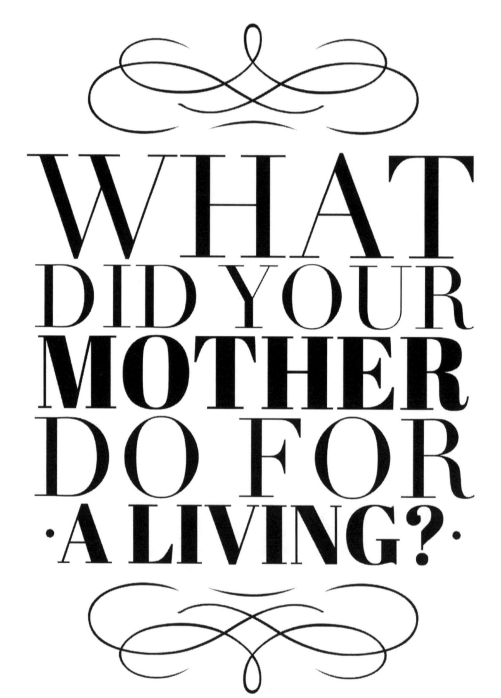

WHAT DID YOUR MOTHER DO FOR A LIVING?

WHAT
DID YOUR
FATHER
·DO FOR·
·A LIVING?·

WHO WERE SOME OF YOUR FAVOURITE RELATIVES, AND WHAT MADE THEM SPECIAL?

· WHAT DO YOU REMEMBER ABOUT YOUR GRANDPARENTS?

· WHAT · DID YOUR GRANDPARENTS · DO FOR A · LIVING?

WHAT WERE YOUR · FAVOURITE CHILDHOOD GAMES OR TOYS?

WHEN YOU WERE A CHILD, WHAT DID YOU WANT TO BE WHEN YOU GREW UP?

WHAT IS YOUR FAVOURITE BOOK?

WHAT IS YOUR FAVOURITE COLOUR?

WHAT IS YOUR ·FAVOURITE· FOOD?

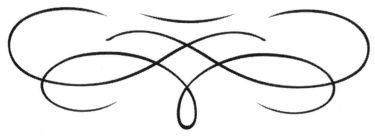

·WHAT IS YOUR·
·FAVOURITE·
QUOTE?

WHO WAS THE BEST TEACHER YOU HAD? WHY?

WHAT ·SPORT· DID ·YOU PLAY· GROWING UP?

·WHAT IS·
·YOUR FAVOURITE·
SPORT?
WHAT TEAM DO YOU SUPPORT?

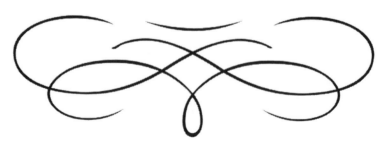

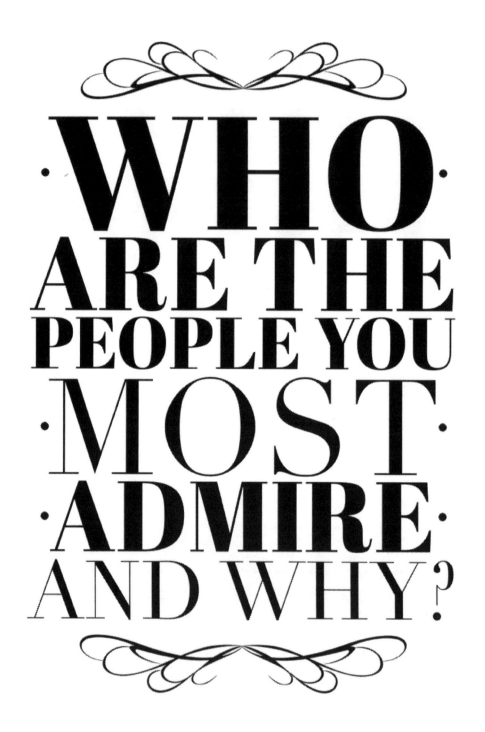

WHO ARE THE PEOPLE YOU MOST ADMIRE AND WHY?

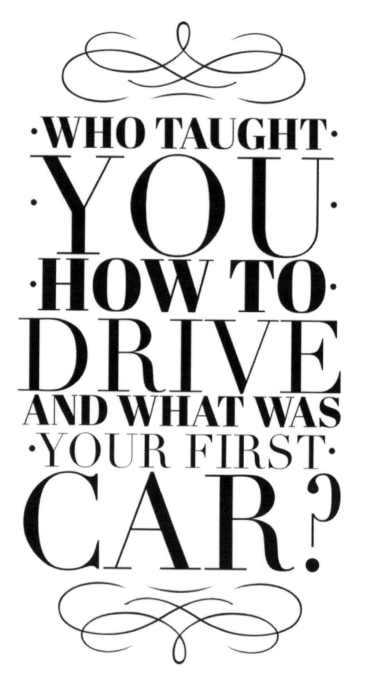

WHO TAUGHT YOU HOW TO DRIVE AND WHAT WAS YOUR FIRST CAR?

WHAT WAS YOUR FIRST JOB AND HOW MUCH DID YOU EARN?

·WHAT MUSIC DID· YOU GROW UP LISTENING TO?

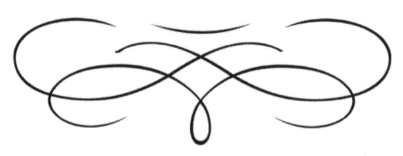

WHO WERE ·YOUR BEST· FRIENDS DURING CHILDHOOD?

WHAT RESPONSIBILITIES DID YOU HAVE AT HOME WHEN YOU WERE YOUNG?

WHAT ARE YOUR ·FAVOURITE· FAMILY RECIPES?

WHAT WAS · YOUR · FIRST DATE LIKE?

HOW DID YOU SPEND YOUR TIME BEFORE YOU HAD CHILDREN?

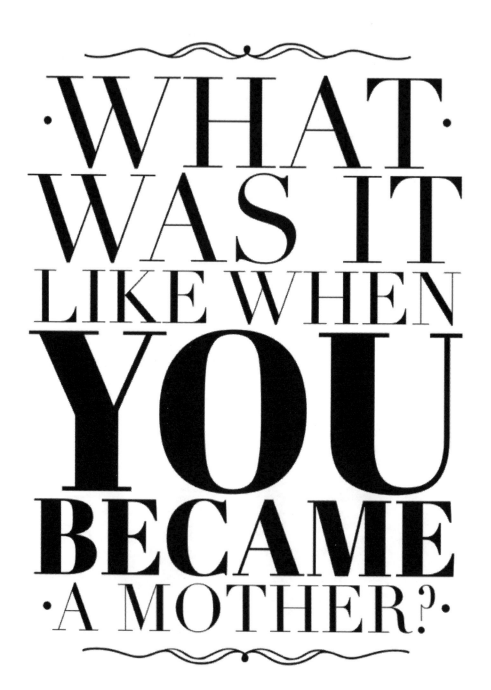

WHAT WAS IT LIKE WHEN YOU BECAME ·A MOTHER?·

WHAT ARE YOUR ·FONDEST· MEMORIES OF YOUR CHILDREN?

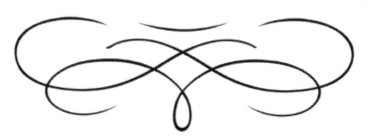

· WHAT DO · YOU REMEMBER ·FOLLOWING· THE BIRTH OF YOUR CHILDREN?

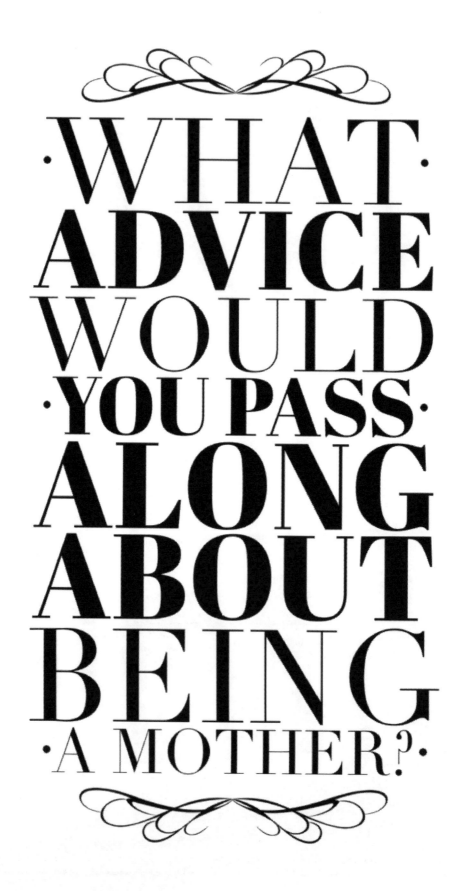

WHAT
TRADITIONS DO
YOU PASSED
DOWN TO
YOUR FUTURE
·GENERATIONS?·

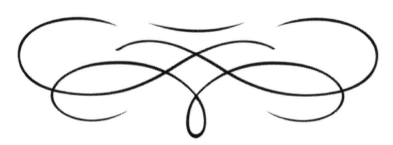

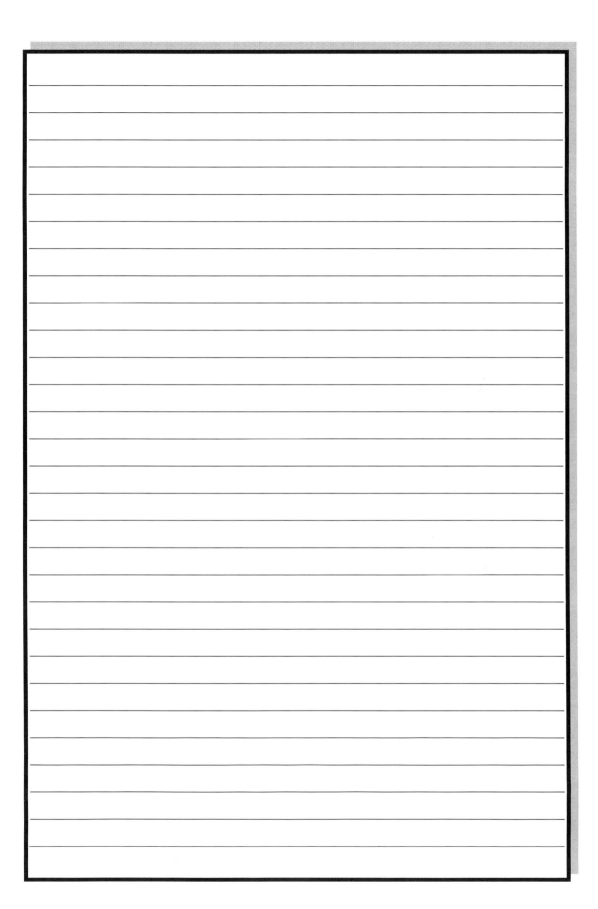

WHAT IS
·THE MOST·
IMPULSIVE THING
YOU HAVE DONE?

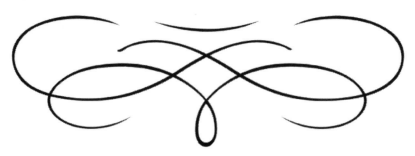

WHERE IS THE
•MOST INTERESTING•
PLACE YOU
HAVE VISITED?

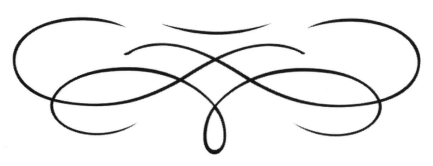

WHAT ARE SOME WAYS- GOOD OR BAD ·THAT THE· ·WORLD HAS· ·CHANGED· SINCE YOU WERE A CHILD?

WHAT DO YOU · KNOW NOW, · · THAT YOU · WISHED YOU · HAD KNOWN WHEN · YOU WERE · YOUNGER?·

IF YOU COULD GO BACK TO ANY AGE WHAT AGE WOULD IT BE? WHY?

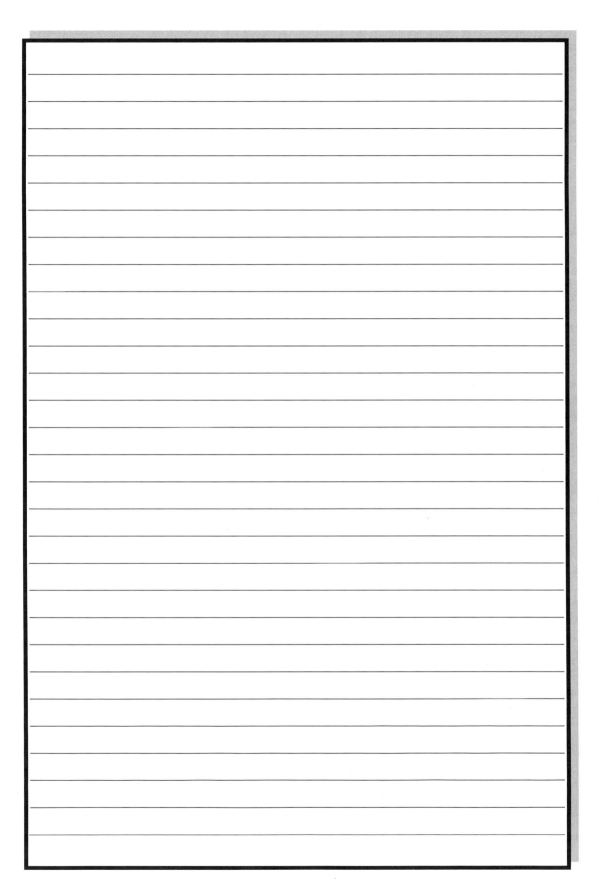

WHAT DO YOU LOOK FORWARD TO NOW?

· IF YOU COULD ·
HAVE
THREE
WISHES
WHAT
· WOULD ·
THEY BE?

HOW HAVE YOUR
•DREAMS OR GOALS•
CHANGED
THROUGHOUT
YOUR LIFE?
DID YOU
ACHIEVE ANY?

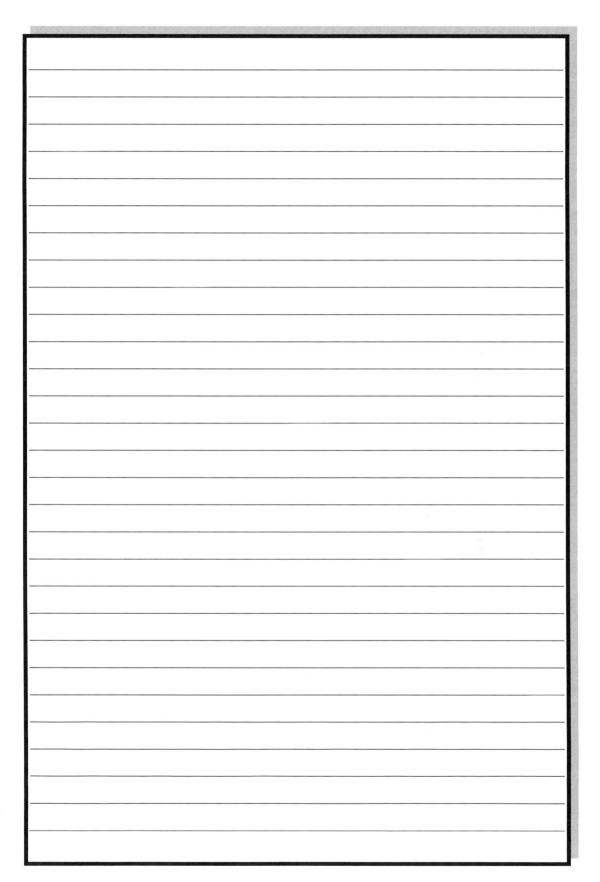

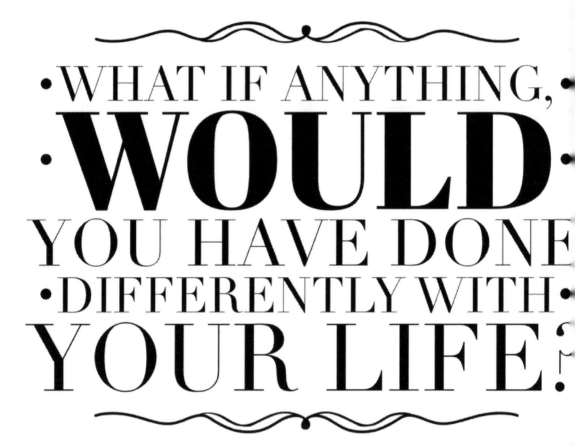

• WHAT IF ANYTHING, •
• **WOULD** •
YOU HAVE DONE
• DIFFERENTLY WITH •
YOUR LIFE?

WHAT BIG WORLD EVENTS WERE
• **THE MOST MEMORABLE** •
WHILE YOU WERE GROWING

UP?

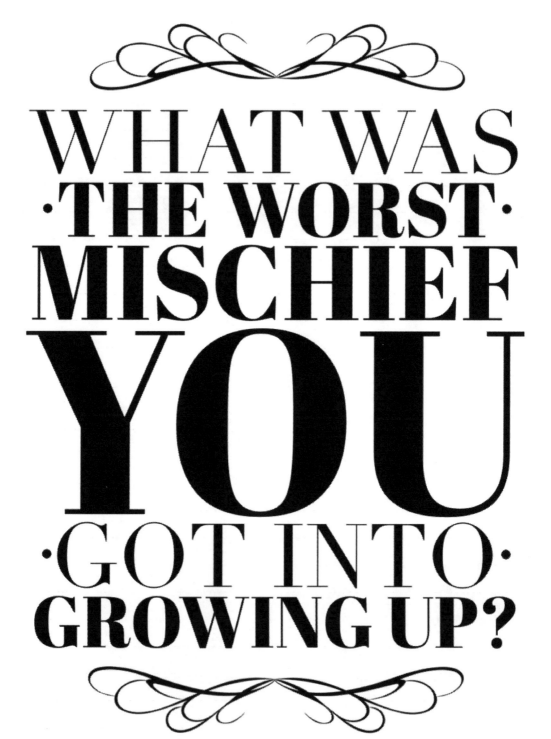

WHAT WAS ·THE WORST· MISCHIEF YOU ·GOT INTO· GROWING UP?

WHAT IS YOUR FAVOURITE PHRASE?

WHAT IS YOUR FAVOURITE TV SHOW?

WHAT DO YOU · LIKE DOING WITH YOUR SPARE TIME!

·DID YOU·
HAVE ANY PETS
GROWING UP? WHAT WERE
·THEIR NAMES?·

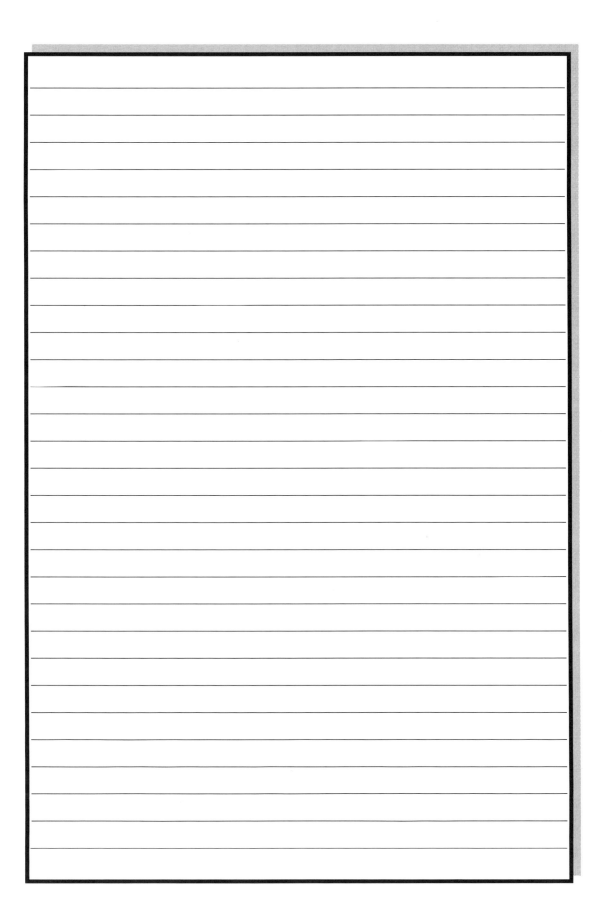

WHAT AWARDS HAVE YOU · WON IN · YOUR LIFETIME?

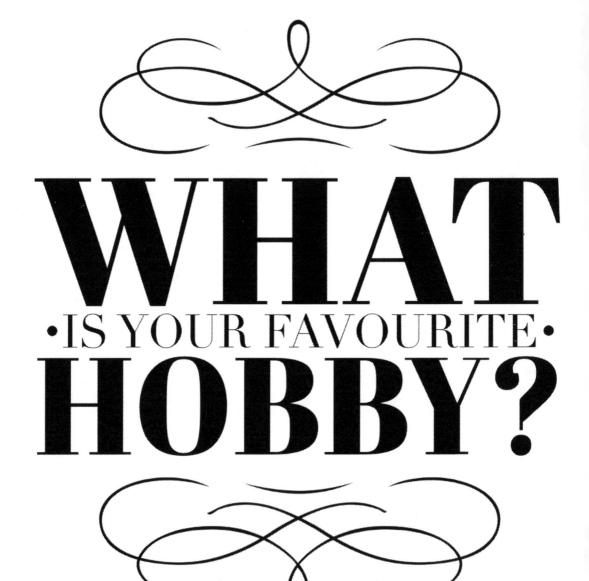

WHAT ·IS YOUR FAVOURITE· HOBBY?

WHAT IS YOUR BEST ATTRIBUTE?

WHAT MAKES ·YOU LAUGH?·

WHAT DO YOU WANT TO BE REMEMBERED FOR?

YOU WILL COME
TO KNOW THAT WHAT APPEARS TODAY TO

be a sacrifice will

PROVE TO INSTEAD

BE

THE GREATEST INVESTMENT THAT
YOU WILL EVER MAKE.

Gordon B. Hinckley

love you mom x

Made in the USA
Lexington, KY
09 May 2019